# FACE TO FACE | EXTREME ANIMALS

# Face to Face WOLVES

### TO FACE

**Jim and Judy Brandenburg**

NATIONAL GEOGRAPHIC
WASHINGTON, D.C.

← If you want to follow wolves in the wild, you have to think like a wolf.

# FACE TO FACE

← Wolves are very aware of their surroundings. Most of the time they are watching you before you see them.

I grew up on the flat and treeless prairie. That's where I first began dreaming about seeing a wild wolf. Wolves were my favorite animals as a boy, even though they were extinct on the prairie. I had seen them only in photos and paintings. When I was finally old enough to drive, I set out for the North Woods of Minnesota. I knew wolves still lived there, and I hoped to photograph one. But I could not find any in the deep, dense woods. They were there, of course, but I didn't know how to look for them.

## WHAT BIG EYES YOU HAVE!

Throughout history, wolves have inspired both fear and admiration. They have been our hunting partners, our competitors, and our guides. This is why nearly every culture has folk stories about wolves.

- Fairy tales like Little Red Riding Hood reflect the fear that Europeans felt for wolves.

- In Rudyard Kipling's *The Jungle Book* and in the myth of Romulus and Remus, baby boys were raised by wolves.

- To some Native Americans, wolves were spirit guides who were revered for their hunting abilities.

Years later, I jumped at the chance to travel to the high Arctic, far north in Canada, for National Geographic. The white wolves there are usually not afraid of people, since they see so few humans. They are curious about us.

When I arrived on Ellesmere Island, just west of Greenland, I saw my first pack of seven white arctic wolves. I followed them as they headed toward an iceberg. The leader of the pack was the first to see me. He looked at me without fear, letting me know there was no way I would sneak up on him. He went on walking and climbing to what was clearly his favorite spot on the iceberg, a shelf halfway up. He sat down to watch me still clumsily trying to catch up to him. When I got as close to him as I could, we stared at each other. I looked at him through my powerful telephoto lens. After all these years, I was finally face to face with my favorite animal.

During that first summer, the wolves became used to seeing me around. I felt like I was part of the pack. I was able to follow them as they hunted musk oxen and then brought the food back to feed their pups, six cute little waddling gray bundles of fur. I watched the pups romp and play.

I left the Arctic after three summers, sad to go but excited, too. I would take what I had learned about wolf behavior and begin looking for gray wolves in my new home, the Boundary Waters Canoe Area Wilderness in northern Minnesota—the wolf country of my boyhood dreams. My wife and co-author, Judy, and I have lived in this beautiful, wild place for 30 years—with wolves for neighbors.

⬆ High on his iceberg throne, the leader of the pack surveys his territory. I named him Buster, after my father, the leader of my family's pack.

A young wolf pup explores his surroundings after his mother moved the pups to a new area, out in the open.

# MEET THE WOLF

That photograph of the wolf on the iceberg turned out to be the most important picture I would ever make. I shot six frames before Buster left, but because of the cold, and my nervousness, only one turned out the way I hoped. Since then, I've learned more about wolves and how to gain their trust.

There are two species of wolves in North America: the red wolf and the most common, the gray wolf *(Canis lupus)*. Gray wolves live around the world, primarily in the northern climates.

A wolf howls to communicate with the rest of the pack. The sound can be heard many miles away.

9

The resident wolf pack in my backyard in Minnesota. Just 35 years ago, when I started photographing them, wolves were one of the most hated animals in the world. Today, they are one of the most loved. My photographs may have helped change attitudes—when you do something you care about, you can really make a difference!

Wolf families are called packs. The pack consists of a mother and father, called the alpha pair, and their offspring. The alpha female and alpha male are the leaders of the pack. The pups usually stay with the pack for two or three years. When they are grown, one of them might become the pack leader—or the alpha pair might drive them away. They then become lone wolves, who may someday join with other lone wolves to mate and form new packs.

The average wolf pack is 6 to 8 wolves. A pack of 20 wolves, including 5 pups, recently lived near me in northern Minnesota. This unusually large pack eventually split. The alpha pair remained nearby, and the new pack went off to set up its own territory. Wolves are territorial. They will travel great distances, about 30 miles (48 km) a day, to patrol their boundaries and to find food.

⬇ Wolves used to live all over the world, in North America, Asia, and Europe. The map below shows the range of the gray and red wolf species today. (The arctic wolf is a subspecies of gray.)

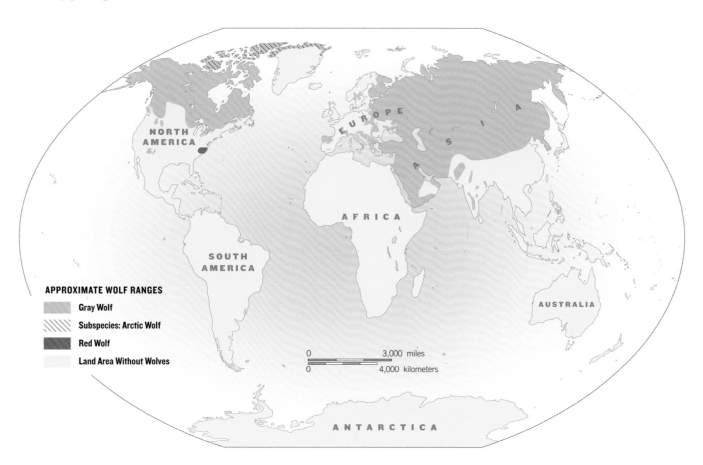

**APPROXIMATE WOLF RANGES**

Gray Wolf

Subspecies: Arctic Wolf

Red Wolf

Land Area Without Wolves

➡ Wolves seem to be always on the move, mostly searching for food. But they are also on the lookout for danger. They can be killed if they wander into another pack's territory. Humans, and their traps, pose another threat.

⬆ The low spring sun highlights the thick winter fur of this arctic wolf.

The coloration of a gray wolf can range from black to white, with many shades of a blondish, gray-brown in between.

## HOW TO SPEAK WOLF

Wolves are famous for howling, but they communicate in lots of other ways, too. They growl, whimper, and use body language.

- A wolf greeting a more dominant animal slinks along the ground and sometimes rolls over on its back. The dominant wolf holds its tail high.

- To show affection, wolves lick each other's muzzles or wag their tails.

- When a wolf stares another wolf in the eye, it's a sign of aggression.

Wolves are social animals, which means they live and cooperate with other wolves. They have many ways to communicate. Smells, sounds, facial expressions, and body language can relay messages.

A wolf howl is one of nature's most interesting sounds. Wolves greet one another, show their location, and define their territory by howling. They can track the rest of the pack and warn off others.

Wolves sleep as much as 12 hours at a time. Upon waking, one wolf howls to the others to wake them up. The rest of the adults slowly get up, stretch, bow to each other, howl, and then depart on their hunt. I love being awakened at night by the sound of a wolf pack howling nearby.

← Pups love to join the rest of the pack in howling, but do so at a higher pitch.

# LIFE IN THE PACK

S cientists often compare the wolf pack to a human family, because wolves live together and care for one another, just like humans. The wolf pack in my backyard has often seemed like family to me. This spring, when I realized that two of the pack's wolf pups had died, I felt the loss strongly.

Each year, around April or May, the alpha female usually bears one litter of four to six pups. Wolf pups weigh one pound at birth and are blind, deaf, and completely dependent on their mother. They

← The pack often leaves the pups in the care of a baby-sitter. This wolf's job is not just to play with and protect them, but to teach important lessons about being a wolf.

**15**

live in a hole or cave that the alpha pair finds or has dug in the ground. This first home is called a den. The pups stay in or near the den until they are about two months old and big enough to travel. Then the adults take them to a new place. This larger, open area, known as a rendezvous site, gives the growing pups more room to explore and sleep. The pups are moved often, and the sites are usually located near food and water sources.

Wolf pups love to play; they stalk, pounce, wrestle, and chew on each other. This is good practice for when they are old enough to go along

The alpha pair always eats first, then the subordinates eat. The wolf with the least status, the omega wolf, eats last.

on hunts with the pack. During play, the pups find out who is the most dominant. This is very important for the stability of the family.

Every adult in the wolf pack will help take care of the pups by bringing them food and playing with them. When most of the pack is out hunting, one adult—the babysitter—usually stays with the pups. Sometimes, if the pack is small, the adults may have to leave the pups alone while they hunt. This leaves the pups vulnerable to other predators, such as bears.

The pack will also share in caring for elder or injured members of the pack. I've watched the pack near my home take care of a wolf I call Broken

⬆ Born with black fuzzy fur, pups nurse until they are about six weeks old.

Much tenderness is shown between the alpha pair during courtship (left).

An adult wolf (left) shows the alpha male it accepts its higher status by displaying submissive body language.

Wolves howl (right) at different pitches to create discord. The pack then appears much larger to other wolf packs in the area.

Foot. One of his front paws was clearly broken and never healed, most likely from a steel trap. For the last three years, he has hopped along on three legs. Other wolves in his pack greet him and show him respect, letting him eat with the pack. Because of his broken foot, he cannot go on a hunt for large animals. But he can hunt small animals like mice by pouncing on them and pinning them.

Wolves are good at catching and killing large animals. They can run very fast, from 25 to 40 miles an hour (40–65 km/h) for short distances. Their powerful jaws and interlocking teeth help them

Hungry pups nip and nuzzle at an adult's mouth to stimulate regurgitation.

## HUNGRY LIKE A WOLF

As predators, wolves actually help deer and other herds stay healthy.

- **Wolfing food:** Wolves tend to prey on animals that are weak. They are easiest to catch!

- **Wolf workout:** The strong, healthy animals are the ones that get away. They survive and reproduce.

- **Cry for the wolf:** When wolves disappear from an area, deer and other animal populations get too numerous and soon suffer from hunger or disease.

catch and hang on to their prey. A wolf pack works together to hunt large prey such as deer, moose, caribou, musk oxen, bison, and elk. A lone wolf will seek out smaller animals like beaver, rabbits, and rodents, which are easier to catch.

To be healthy, each wolf should have about 2.5 pounds of food a day, so wolves must hunt often to catch enough food for the pack. They tend to prey on the sick, weak, injured, old, or young. When hunting is poor, wolves can go for long periods without eating. Especially for pups, starvation is one of the main causes of death. 🐾

A volunteer carries a sedated pup in Yellowstone National Park, Wyoming. The pup, which came from Canada, would eventually be released into the park.

# MAKING A COMEBACK

An arctic wolf jumps from one ice floe to another in search of scraps of food washed up from the sea.

In the early 1970s, there were fewer than 1,000 gray and red wolves left in the lower 48 states. To protect wolves from further decline, they were two of the first species given protection under the Endangered Species Act of 1973.

Since then, the wolf has made a remarkable recovery. How many wolves are there now in the world? Some estimates show more than 5,000 wolves in the lower 48 states, including 2,000 in Minnesota, and 7,000 to 12,000 in Alaska.

Worldwide, there are at least 150,000 in 57 different countries.

Scientists have many ongoing studies of the wolf. The longest study of the wolf-and-prey relationship is at Isle Royale National Park on Lake Superior, where scientists have been observing wolves and their relationship with moose for 50 years.

In 1995 and 1996, wild wolves from Canada were released, or reintroduced, in the northern Rocky Mountains of Yellowstone National Park and in Idaho. Yellowstone is now the best place to

see and hear wild wolves.

Local ranchers were opposed to the wolf reintroductions and threatened to shoot them to prevent
them from attacking livestock. A group called
Defenders of Wildlife worked out a compromise.
They established a fund to pay farmers and ranchers for livestock that the wolves killed. However, it's
not always clear how the livestock died. Wolves
often eat animals that have died from other causes.

America's wolves still need our help. Some
people want to change the wolves' status. In

↑ Here I am, following wolf
tracks and hoping to find
a wolf pack in Minnesota's
Boundary Waters Canoe Area
Wilderness.

Once highly endangered, wolves have made a remarkable recovery over the past 25 years. Here, a lone wolf howls to find his pack on Ellesmere Island, Canada.

Minnesota, wolf populations have begun to recover. Wolves in this state are no longer on the endangered species list.

In Alaska, where wolves were never endangered, they are hunted from airplanes. And new laws in Montana and Idaho allow hunters to kill hundreds of wolves. Environmental groups are speaking out against this change. Why is there a rush to kill these wolves? One reason is that wolves are often blamed for the decline in populations of elk and other animals hunted for sport, even though these declines may be also caused by natural events, like drought, or even human hunters.

People's fear and misunderstanding of wolves is the biggest threat to their survival. I hope that this attitude will change, and the howl of the wolf will again be heard in places it used to call home.

# HOW YOU CAN HELP

⬇ Two young wolf pups play tug-of-war with a piece of fur from an arctic fox.

Humans and wolves in North America have had a long, tangled relationship. Many Native American tribes respected and revered wolves. But European settlers had a different view. As settlers pushed west in the 1800s, they came into conflict with wolves, who sometimes hunted their domestic animals. The federal government began paying hunters a bounty—a sum of money—for every wolf they killed. Wolves were shot, poisoned, and trapped to the brink of extinction.

That view of wolves has changed. Wolves were added to the endangered species list in 1973, and since then, wolf populations have made a comeback.

But some hunters and ranchers continue to oppose wolf reintroductions and laws that protect wolves. They blame wolves for a decline in deer herds, even though the decline could be caused by other factors, including drought, disease, and overhunting by humans. Other people think wolves are dangerous to humans, but healthy wild wolves have rarely attacked humans in North America. Wolves are legally hunted in Alaska, and other states are trying to pass laws to allow hunting.

Here's how you can help:

■ Be a wolf ambassador. Help to educate others about the important role wolves play in the ecosystem. Remind them that in modern times, there is not a single proven case of a wild, healthy wolf killing a person in the U.S.

■ Learn about organizations like Defenders of Wildlife, the Wolf Conservation Center, and the International Wolf Center, which protect wild wolves.

■ You and your friends or family could "adopt" a wolf from Wolf Song of Alaska or Defenders of Wildlife. In return, you might get a certificate or a wolf toy. Plus, you'll feel good knowing that you are helping protect wolves.

■ Write to your representatives in Congress, especially if you live in a state that has wolves. Tell them that wild wolves are important to you and you want them protected.

# IT'S YOUR TURN

Unless you live in the northern woods of Minnesota like Jim Brandenburg, you may have a hard time finding wolves in the wild. Here are some ideas for how you can enjoy wolves:

**1** You might get a chance to see a wolf—or hear their haunting howls—if your family takes a trip to Yellowstone National Park in Wyoming. You could also see a wolf at a zoo or wildlife park. Some zoos keep wolves in family groups, where you can see them interact. How would the behavior of captive wolves be different from that of wild ones? How would it be the same?

**2** There are many websites where you can listen to wolf howls. Try www.pbs.org/wgbh/nova/wolves/howl.html and www.wolfpark.org/animals/sounds.

**3** Pay attention to the body language of the family dog. Wild wolves are its ancestors! Just like wolves, dogs roll over on their backs to show submission to a dominant member of their pack, wave their tails in greeting, and bow down and slap the ground with their forelegs when they want to play.

**4** Curl up with a good book. You might like *Julie of the Wolves* by Jean Craighead George. This classic story is about a young girl who spends a season living with a family of arctic wolves. What typical wolf behaviors are described?

**5** *Never Cry Wolf* is a movie about a wolf biologist who goes to the Arctic to solve the mystery of why caribou are dying. Based on a true story, it helped to dispel myths about wolves and to change people's attitudes toward them.

⬇ As pups grow, they become very curious about their surroundings.

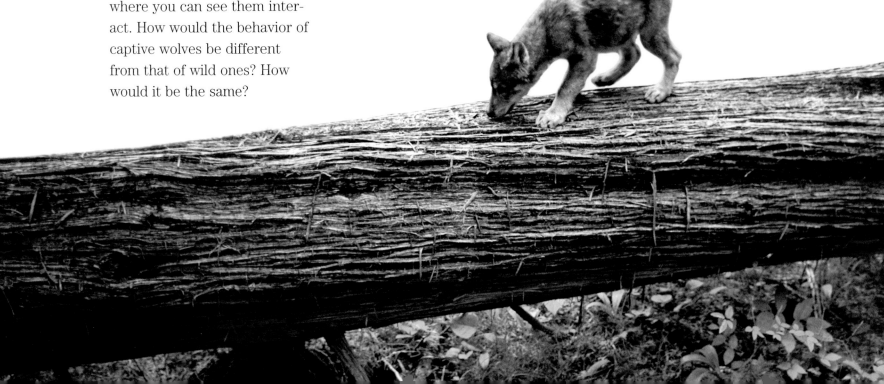

# FACTS AT A GLANCE

⬇ An arctic wolf rests in a field of cotton grass after a long hunt; wolves sometimes sleep 12 hours straight.

### ▰ Scientific and Common Names

The species name for the gray wolf is *Canis lupus.* The gray wolf has five subspecies in North America: the arctic wolf, the eastern timber wolf, the Rocky Mountain or Mackenzie Valley wolf, the Mexican wolf, and the Great Plains wolf. All canines (wolves, dogs, foxes, jackals, and coyotes) belong to a group of animals called Carnivora, which also includes bears, seals, and other predators.

### ▰ Types of Wolves

There are two wolf species: gray and red. (Another animal, the Ethiopian wolf, is considered a third, separate species of wolf by many scientists. However, others argue that it is just related to wolves, like a jackal or coyote is.) At least 150,000 gray wolves exist; they are not endangered. Red wolves, native to the southeastern United States, are critically endangered, with fewer than 150 animals.

### ▰ Size

Gray wolves are the largest canines in the wild, standing 26–32 inches (66–81 cm) tall at the shoulder. On average, females weigh about 80 pounds (36 kg); males about 90 pounds (41 kg).

### ▰ Life Spans

It's tough being a wolf. Young wolves die from starvation or are killed by predators like bears, coyotes, or other wolves. Grown wolves can starve or suffer from diseases, be killed by hunters, be hit by cars, or be injured by the flying hooves of their prey. The average wild wolf lives six to eight years. Captive wolves can live for twice as long.

### ▰ Special Features

Wolves are intelligent and highly social creatures. They communicate through sound, scent marking, and body language. Within the pack, social status determines which wolves get such privileges as eating first or mating. Groups of wolves hunt cooperatively to capture prey.

### ▰ Habitat and Range

Wolves used to live in northern

**Approximate Gray Wolf Range**

UNITED STATES

Map A: Historic Range

Map B: 1973 Range

Map C: Current Range

latitudes around the world. They are adapted to many environments, including prairie, woods, desert, and arctic regions. Now they live mainly in remote wilderness areas in Canada, the northern United States, and parts of Europe and Asia.

### Food

Wolves hunt a variety of prey, from huge caribou and moose to tiny field mice. Occasionally, they are scavengers, eating animals that are already dead. Sometimes wolves kill cattle and sheep, leading to conflicts with humans. Wolves live in a perpetual cycle of feasting and famine. A wolf can gulp 20 pounds (9 kg) of meat at a sitting, or it can go two weeks without eating.

### Reproduction

Wolves usually live in family groups consisting of an alpha pair of wolves who reproduce, and several other wolves who may be grown offspring from previous years or other relatives. Wolves mate between January and May, depending on where they live, and the pups are born after a 60-day gestation (pregnancy). Pups don't open their eyes until they are two weeks old. They usually come out of the den for the first time at three weeks of age. They join the pack on the hunt when they are about six months old.

### Biggest Threats

Because wolves need large territories in order to find enough food, habitat loss is a serious

⬆ Before Europeans settled the U.S., gray wolves lived in most of the country (Map A). By 1973, when they were listed as endangered, gray wolves were practically extinct in the U.S., living only in a limited area of northeastern Minnesota and Michigan's Isle Royale (Map B). Today, gray wolf populations are recovering as a result of their protected status and their reintroduction to selected areas (Map C).

problem for them. So is illegal killing by human hunters and ranchers. Where the needs of wolves and humans conflict, humans are the biggest threat that wolves have.

**29**

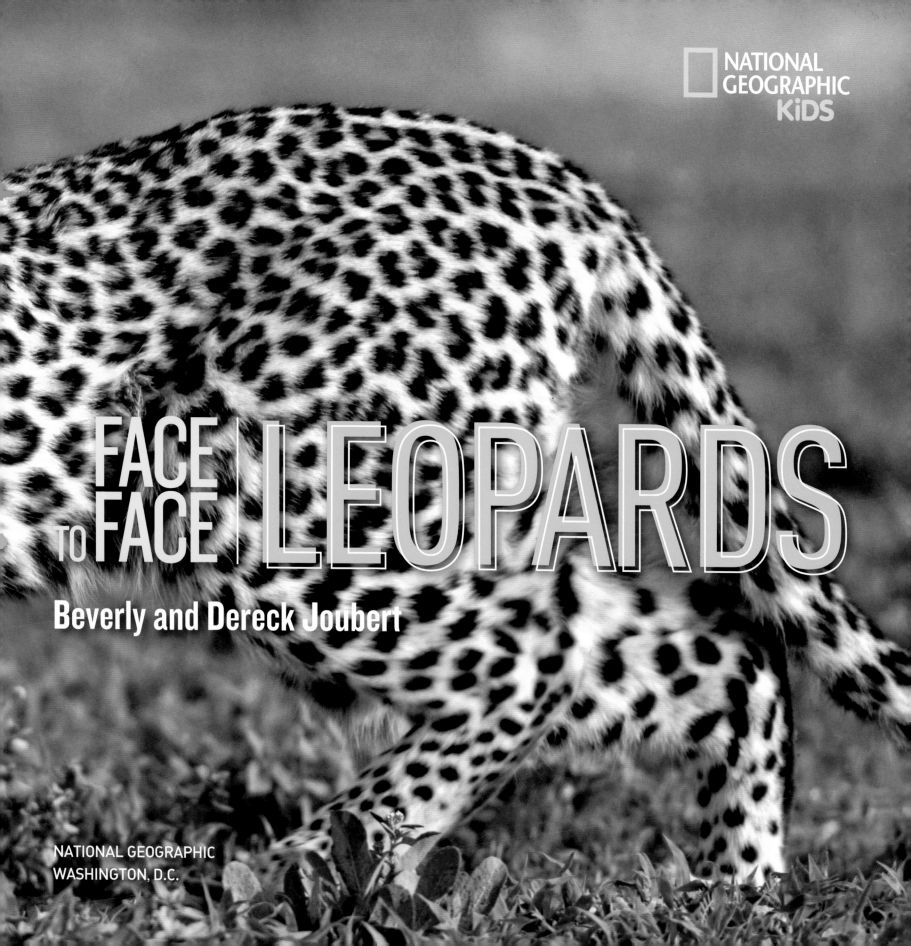

NATIONAL GEOGRAPHIC
WASHINGTON, D.C.

# Face to Face LEOPARDS

Beverly and Dereck Joubert

We've known this leopard, whom we call Legadema, since she was a cub. When she saw her own reflection in my lens, she wanted to play.

# FACE TO FACE

Leopards have eyes like honey and teeth like needles. Their whiskers are very sensitive.

It's not easy to come face to face with a leopard. They are usually shy and secretive. But this one was only eight days old when we spotted her. She seemed curious and bold. And back then, she didn't look fierce at all—more like a fat house cat.

My wife, Beverly, and I have been filming and photographing African wildlife for many years. We were in the Okavango Delta, in Botswana, when we first saw this leopard baby.

As we admired the cub, her mother looked up and

bared her teeth at us. She arched her back and came toward us. We were sitting in our jeep, which doesn't have any doors. They get in the way when we're filming. Now I wondered if that was such a good idea!

Growling, the mother leopard smelled the front of the vehicle. When she came around to my side, our eyes met. Her mouth was full of foamy spit and needle-sharp teeth. I froze. She hissed. Then she turned and went back to her cub. For the next four years, Beverly and I followed that cub as she grew up. The mother leopard never hissed at us again.

About three months later, a thunderstorm broke out while the cub's mother was out hunting. Alone, the cub shivered with fear. It was her first storm. Suddenly, lightning struck the tree next to us.

I thought the cub would run away. But instead, she ran straight toward us and crouched by my feet! After that, people started calling her Legadema (pronounced LACH-ah-DEE-ma). In the local language of Botswana, that means "light from above," or lightning.

Legadema became a kind of friend to us. But we kept our distance. It can be dangerous for leopards and humans to get too close. 🐾

# MEET THE LEOPARD

One day Legadema was in a curious mood. She had been watching us as we worked in the jeep. When Beverly moved to the back of the car, Legadema came up to the vehicle. Then she climbed into Beverly's seat and looked me right in the face!

We were amazed, but we knew we had to discourage this behavior. It could be a disaster if Legadema tried it with tourists visiting the game reserve. I decided to teach her some manners the same way her mother would. I hissed at her. She

A leopard's spots and color give it the perfect camouflage.

As the mother leopard licks her cub, she protects the cub from infection. The mom's spit, or saliva, is like an antiseptic.

ignored me. Then I turned on the car heater, which made a more impressive noise. That made her leave.

Legadema is unusual. Most leopards avoid humans, although some have been known to attack and kill people. But usually these big cats

prefer other prey, such as antelope and deer.

Leopards are solitary animals. This means they spend most of their lives alone. Except for mating, they avoid other leopards. It's rare to see more than one leopard at a time unless it is a mother and cubs.

Leopard cubs stay with their mothers for about two years. They have a lot to learn in that time. They watch their mothers hunt. They learn which trees are best to hide in and which trunks are easy to climb.

One day, Legadema's mom brought her a present. It was an impala, a type of antelope. Legadema played with it by chasing it and pouncing on it. This game helped her practice the hunting skills she would need to survive on her own one day.

When Legadema was about 13 months old, her mother chased her away. The young leopard had been killing her own food for a while, so her mom must have known she was ready. Legadema wandered around by herself, touching and sniffing each of her mother's favorite trees. She hunted small animals. Her mother seemed to give her some space in their territory. We think she may even have been watching over Legadema and keeping in touch by scent and markings rather than by actually meeting.

When cats lift their young, the cubs freeze. You probably shouldn't wriggle too much when mom's sharp teeth are around your neck!

◀ A sausage tree provides the perfect fortress for Legadema and her mom. It has lots of deep holes to hide in, and the cub can dig her claws in its soft bark and climb.

➡ After a hard night of hunting, mom just wants to rest, but Legadema has other ideas.

Over time, Legadema found her place in the leopard world as an adult. Now she, too, is a mother.

But she hasn't forgotten us. We had been away for a while and then went back for a visit. As soon as Legadema spotted us, she came over to the car. She looked up into Beverly's eyes. Then she circled over to me and sniffed my shoe. Soon she was lying in the shade under our jeep, just like she used to. 🐾

Leopards catch their prey off guard by leaping to the ground from high up in the trees.

# FOREST GHOSTS

Leopards prowl the forest like ghosts. They slip through the shadows. They slink through tall grass. Even in bright sunlight, it's hard to see them. Their yellowish fur with dark spots blends into the background. This helps them hide from their prey until they are ready to pounce.

Like all big cats, leopards are predators. This means they hunt, kill, and eat other animals to survive. Leopards eat almost anything they can

This vervet monkey was just a little too slow and couldn't escape a sly leopard.

catch, from birds to monkeys to Cape buffalo. Almost nothing is safe!

The leopard hunts alone. It creeps up on its prey secretly and silently. This is called stalking. We have watched a leopard lie in wait for hours, watching an antelope nibble grass. Slowly, the

A leopard's powerful jaw muscles and sharp claws help it drag an impala up a tree, away from other predators that might steal it.

powerful cat inches closer and closer, until—
*wham!* It springs at its prey, pins the animal
down, and kills it, usually with one fierce bite.

Instead of eating their catch on the spot,
leopards often drag it away. They do this to get
away from the lions and hyenas that might steal
their meal. They stash it under a bush or haul it
up into the treetops. A leopard is so strong that
it can drag an animal twice its weight up a tree.
It does this with the help of its powerful neck,
shoulder, and jaw muscles and its strong legs.

Besides being good climbers, leopards are also
strong swimmers. They will catch and eat fish,
crabs, and other water animals—even small hippos!

Leopards have sharp eyesight and keen hear-
ing, which help them detect prey. They usually
hunt at night. But at Mombo, the region in the
Okavango Delta where Legadema lives, we saw
her hunt during the day and night.

To us it looks like leopards really have fun
sometimes. An adult leopard might spot a
squirrel and spend an hour chasing it up and
down trees, over logs, and in and out of holes.
I think the big cat must enjoy the chase, since

⬆ Predators eat meat, and
they have to kill in order to
survive. Predators and prey
are a natural part of life in
the wild.

**45**

# CAN A LEOPARD CHANGE **HIS SPOTS?**

Telling one leopard from another seems hard. Here are some ways researchers "spot" the difference!

■ On the fat upper lip on either side of a leopard's nose are rows of dark black spots with a whisker coming out of each. The pattern of these whisker spots is different for each cat.

■ Every leopard also has a unique pattern of dark spots around its neck. This band of black spots is called a necklace. In addition, researchers often use the spots on the sides of leopards' bodies to identify them.

■ As a cub, Legadema had a unique spot on her upper lip that was a perfect way to identify her. She still has it today, which shows that a leopard really does not change its spots!

the small mouthful of fur doesn't seem like much of a reward for all that effort.

Sometimes leopards stalk and prey on baboons. But sometimes the baboons are the predators. When Legadema was a cub, we saw a troop of baboons try to drag her and her mother out of their den. A mob of baboons can rip a leopard to shreds. Legadema learned to hide or run away when she met a group of them. Lions also pose a danger to leopards. We have seen lions chase a leopard up into a tree and then try to pull it down and kill it.

Smell is important to leopards. They claw tree trunks and spray their urine on trees to leave their scent behind. This tells other leopards that the territory is theirs. This way, they can avoid others. If one leopard does see another, it will usually turn away. Leopards also roar to let other leopards know where they are. A leopard's roar sounds sort of like a deep, raspy cough.

Leopards live in many parts of Africa and Asia. A few leopards appear to be solid black. I once saw one for an instant. Within the black coat there were even darker spots, like a normal leopard has. This is

⬆ Legadema makes a quick exit when she spots these elephants looming over her.

different from what is commonly known as a black panther, which is often a black jaguar or even a dark mountain lion. No matter what their overall color is, leopards are expert at disappearing. It's almost as if they have Harry Potter's invisibility cloak! 🐾

**47**

◀ Legadema scans the tree-tops for squirrels. Hunting them became an obsession for her.

# LEOPARD LEGACY

◀ As a cub, Legadema loved to play. She just had to watch out for her mom's sharp teeth and claws—and that cat breath!

**L**eopards live in more climates and habitats than any other big cat. They live in Africa, Central Asia, India, Russia, and China. They live in forests, grasslands, deserts, and mountains. They survive in warm climates and in cold. In fact, leopards can adapt to nearly any habitat. In some parts of the world, they even live in suburban areas. They just need a place to hide in and hunt.

But even though they are very adaptable, they still face many problems. One of the biggest is habitat loss.

**49**

➡ When there are baboons in the area, Legadema returns to a safe place.

# HOW TO SPOT A BIG CAT BY ITS SPOTS

Leopards aren't the only big cats with spots. Jaguars and cheetahs have them, too. Here's how to spot the difference.

■ A leopard's spots group together to form clusters. These are called rosettes, because they look a bit like a rose. The rosettes do not have a dot in the center.

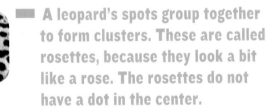

■ The jaguar's coat is patterned with rings of small black spots. The rings are also called rosettes. They often have a black dot in the center.

■ The spots on a cheetah's coat are solid. They are evenly spaced and do not form rosettes.

As human populations grow, we take over land that was once wild, and the animals lose their habitat.

When leopards live near human settlements, they may prey on dogs and on livestock such as cattle and pigs. To protect their animals, farmers shoot, trap, or poison the big cats. In some places, wildlife conservation groups pay cattle owners for livestock that leopards kill, as long as the owners don't kill the cats.

Leopards face another challenge. Some African countries still allow leopard hunting. Leopards are hunted for their valuable fur coats. They are also killed for their tails, claws, and whiskers, which are used in some traditional medicines.

Permits are issued, allowing only a certain number

⬆ She's fully grown now, but we can usually still find Legadema in the same trees she liked to climb as a cub.

of leopards to be hunted worldwide. But we think it's still too many, because no one knows how many are killed by poachers, who hunt illegally, without permits.

Leopards are very difficult to see, let alone count, but we know their numbers are declining. Today, some conservationists think there may be as few as 50,000 mature leopards, but we need more

← Legadema perches
confidently on a branch,
queen of all she surveys.

information. In some parts of the world, especially
Asia, the leopard is already on the verge of extinction.

Leopards play an important role in the wild. Without
the top predators, the number of prey species would go
out of balance. There would be so many prey animals
that soon they would have trouble finding food. They
would damage the environment by eating too much
plant life. So predators are important to the balance of
nature. They prey on the weaker members of a herd,
making the herd stronger. They keep them on the move,
fit and alert, always ready to flee from those spots in the
grass that just might be a leopard in disguise.

Today, many people are turning against hunting, and
many national parks protect the big cats. Tourism also
helps by raising money for conservation and helping
people appreciate wildlife. We are very hopeful that in
time more people will learn to value these precious
animals and that their populations will start to recover. 🐾

# HOW YOU CAN HELP

⬇ Leopards have keen eyesight.

Helping leopards starts with understanding them. Learn all you can about these big cats. You are already off to a good start! Read about leopards in books and magazines and on the Internet. Watch documentary films and TV programs about them. Visit leopards in zoos. The more you learn about leopards, the more you will appreciate them. You might even come to love them as deeply as we do.

Talk to everyone you can about leopards and share what you've learned. Someone who is passionate about something and who knows a lot about the subject can have a lot of influence.

Support conservation groups that protect big cats. For example, the World Wildlife Fund and the African Wildlife Foundation have up-to-date information on leopard conservation on their websites. So does the National Geographic Big Cat Initiative, which we founded. It raises funds for emergency help for lions, leopards, cheetahs, and tigers. And it is working. A few years ago, when we started the program, one area in Kenya was losing 40 lions a year and countless leopards. A year later, the program had helped limit the losses to just one lion and no leopards at all.

Think about how to raise money to help conservation organizations keep big cats safe. Rally your classmates, teachers, friends, and families. Encourage them to go on the website of one of these groups and donate whatever they can afford. Every little bit helps to keep these cats from dying out.

You can help preserve the world's wild places for leopards and other wildlife by doing what you can to reduce the impact you have on the natural world each day. Don't waste water. Recycle whatever you can. The fewer forests that are chopped down to make paper products, for example, the more space there will be for all wildlife to survive.

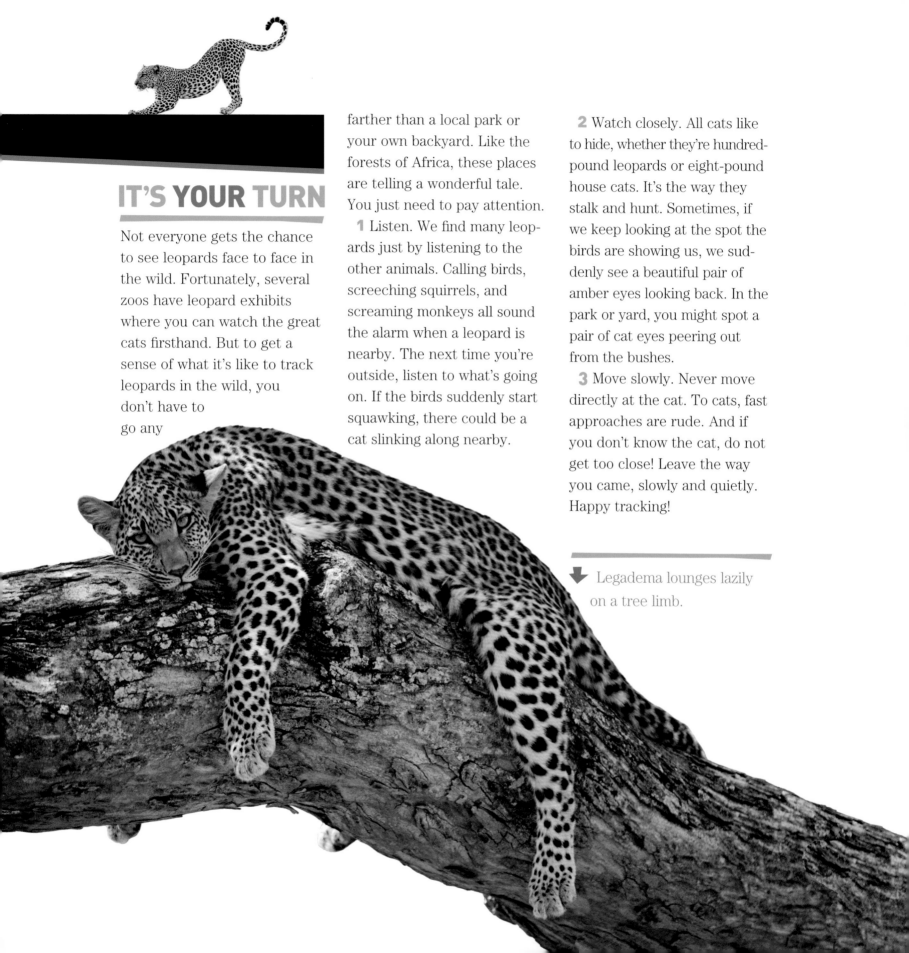

# IT'S **YOUR TURN**

Not everyone gets the chance to see leopards face to face in the wild. Fortunately, several zoos have leopard exhibits where you can watch the great cats firsthand. But to get a sense of what it's like to track leopards in the wild, you don't have to go any farther than a local park or your own backyard. Like the forests of Africa, these places are telling a wonderful tale. You just need to pay attention.

**1** Listen. We find many leopards just by listening to the other animals. Calling birds, screeching squirrels, and screaming monkeys all sound the alarm when a leopard is nearby. The next time you're outside, listen to what's going on. If the birds suddenly start squawking, there could be a cat slinking along nearby.

**2** Watch closely. All cats like to hide, whether they're hundred-pound leopards or eight-pound house cats. It's the way they stalk and hunt. Sometimes, if we keep looking at the spot the birds are showing us, we suddenly see a beautiful pair of amber eyes looking back. In the park or yard, you might spot a pair of cat eyes peering out from the bushes.

**3** Move slowly. Never move directly at the cat. To cats, fast approaches are rude. And if you don't know the cat, do not get too close! Leave the way you came, slowly and quietly. Happy tracking!

Legadema lounges lazily on a tree limb.

# FACTS AT A GLANCE

↓ Legadema and her mom patrol their territory.

### Scientific Name
Leopards belong to the cat family, called Felidae. The species name is *Panthera pardus*.

### Common Name
There are several different varieties, or subspecies, of leopards. Some are named after the place they come from, such as the Chinese leopard, which lives in northern China. Despite their names, the snow leopard *(Panthera uncia)* and the clouded leopard *(Neofelis nebulosa)* are not true leopards.

### Life Span
In the wild, leopards live 12 to 17 years. In captivity they have been known to live 23 years.

### Size
Leopards weigh 66 to 176 pounds (30–80 kg). Males are heavier than females. Leopards vary in length from 3 to 6 feet (91–191 cm); tails are about 23 to 44 inches (58–110 cm) long.

### Diet
Leopards are meat-eaters, or carnivores. They eat a wide variety of animals, including antelope, deer, squirrels and other rodents, birds, monkeys, baboons, fish, reptiles, and porcupines. We have seen them kill 33 species of wildlife in the area of Africa that we study. Leopards also will eat meat killed by other animals. I've even seen a leopard eating an elephant! One day some lions were eating an old elephant when a male leopard snuck in quietly and joined the feast.

### Reproduction
Females are pregnant for about three and a half months before they give birth. They usually have litters of two to three cubs. Life as a baby leopard can be tough. Legadema's mother lost five previous cubs to hyenas, baboons, and other predators before Legadema was born.

### Habitat and Range
These adaptable cats live in a wide variety of habitats—rain forests, open woodlands, dry grasslands, plains, deserts, and mountains. They can survive in cold and warm climates. They live in sub-Saharan Africa, northeast Africa, the Arabian

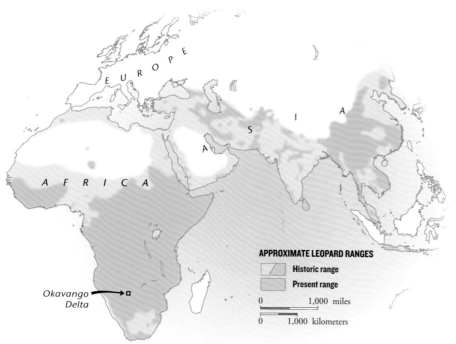

APPROXIMATE LEOPARD RANGES

Historic range

Present range

0       1,000   miles

0       1,000   kilometers

Okavango Delta

EUROPE

ASIA

AFRICA

As the map shows, leopards were once more widely distributed throughout the world than they are today.

Peninsula, the Middle East, Central Asia, India, and China.

### Biggest Threats

Loss of habitat is one of the biggest threats to leopards' survival. Their habitats are being destroyed for logging and farming and to make way for roads and houses. Leopards are also being shot, trapped, or poisoned by farmers who believe the big cats are killing their livestock. Hunters and poachers kill the big cats for sport or for their fur and other body parts.

### Status in the Wild

The number of leopards living in the wild has declined greatly in the last hundred years, and it continues to decrease. Today, some conservationists estimate that about 50,000 mature leopards exist in the wild. While they are still fairly numerous in some places, such as parts of southern Africa, in other places leopards are endangered.

The rarest leopard of all is probably the Amur leopard. It was once found throughout the Korea Peninsula, northeastern China, and southeastern Russia. Now it is extinct in South Korea. Only a handful of Amur leopards are left in the mountainous regions of China and Russia. Researchers estimate that there are fewer than 50 of them living in the wild today.

# POLAR BEARS

## FACE TO FACE

**Norbert Rosing**
**With Elizabeth Carney**

NATIONAL GEOGRAPHIC
WASHINGTON, D.C.

← I'm all bundled up and ready for a long day of photographing polar bears in the icy Arctic.

# FACE TO FACE

← A slumbering giant: Polar bears are one of the largest land carnivores in the world.

One fall, my wife, Elli, and I had a single goal: to photograph polar bears. We were staying at a research camp outside "the polar bear capital of the world"—the town of Churchill, in Manitoba, Canada.

Taking pictures of polar bears is amazing but also dangerous. Polar bears—like all wild animals—should be photographed from a safe distance. When I'm face to face with a polar bear, I like it to be through a camera with a telephoto lens. But sometimes, that is easier said than done. This was one of those times.

## HOW BIG IS THIS BEAR?

- Polar bears are one of the largest land predators in the whole world.

- Paws can be 12 inches (30 cm) across—that's some foot!

- Males may weigh as much as a small car—over 1,700 pounds (770 kg).

- Male bears are as long as normal room height from floor to ceiling.

As Elli and I cooked dinner, a young male polar bear who was playing in a nearby lake sniffed, and smelled our spaghetti and garlic bread.

The hungry bear followed his nose to our camp, which was surrounded by a high, wire fence. He clawed, bit, and shoved the wire mesh. He stood on his hind legs and pushed at the wooden fence posts.

Terrified, Elli and I tried all the bear defense actions we knew. We yelled at the bear, banged pots, and fired blank shotgun shells into the air. Sometimes loud noises like these will scare bears off. Not this polar bear—he just growled and went back to trying to tear down the fence with his massive paws.

I radioed the camp manager for help. He told me a helicopter was on its way, but it would be 30 minutes before it arrived. Making the best of this close encounter, I snapped some pictures of the bear.

Elli and I feared the fence wouldn't last through 30 more minutes of the bear's punishment. The camp manager suggested I use pepper spray. The spray burns the bears' eyes, but doesn't hurt them.

So I crept up to our uninvited guest and, through the fence, sprayed him in the face. With an angry roar, the bear ran back to the lake to wash his eyes.

This young male polar bear tries to push down the fence that circles the camp. He was probably extra hungry because of a toothache, which made it difficult for him to chew. He was hoping for my spaghetti!

A few minutes later, the helicopter arrived. As we were lifted into the air, we saw the stubborn bear was already heading back to our camp.

When Elli and I got home and developed our pictures, we noticed this bear had broken an important tooth. Like humans, polar bears feel pain, have emotions, and can be afraid. Elli and I learned our lesson: Beware of a bear with a toothache.

A mother polar bear sits with her two cubs in Manitoba, Canada. Polar bears most commonly give birth to twins.

# MEET THE POLAR BEAR

I started traveling to the Arctic to photograph wildlife 17 years ago. At first, I planned to photograph things like wildflowers and the northern lights. But my plans changed. I became fascinated with polar bears. The first time I looked into the eyes of a polar bear, I felt an important moment of connection. I knew this was the animal I was destined to capture on film for all to see. Since then, I have had my truck's tires slashed by a polar bear. I nearly lost my fingertips to frostbite. And I narrowly

Like a dog after a bath, a polar bear shakes water from its coat after a swim.

**65**

escaped becoming a bear's lunch after my truck got stuck in a snowdrift. Still, nothing has ruined my feeling of connection to this amazing animal.

Polar bears might look similar to their cousins, the land-dwelling black bears and brown bears. But besides their color, these white bears are different in one big way. Polar bears are marine mammals. Like seals and walruses, they spend most of their lives on the ocean. In fact, their scientific name, *Ursus maritimus,* means "sea bear."

The icy Arctic Ocean and lands that surround the North Pole are a polar bear's idea of paradise. These bears are built to keep warm in freezing temperatures. For much of the year, they spend their days sleeping in snowdrifts and playing and hunting on sea ice.

Polar bears eat mainly the fat and meat of other animals. Seals are their favorite meals. They sometimes eat walruses and caribou, too. I've watched polar bears nab their prey in many different ways. In one common method, the bear stands very still

➡ A bear feasts on one of its favorite meals, a walrus, in Igloolik, Canada. Polar bears don't bury leftovers for later meals the way other bears do.

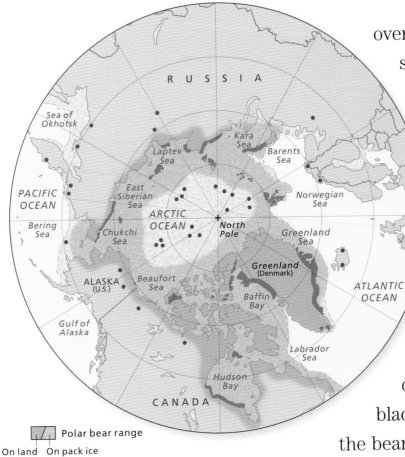

Polar bear range
On land    On pack ice

Polar bear denning sites

Maximum extent of winter pack ice

Country boundary

• Rare polar bear sightings

⬆ Polar bears live in the Arctic, near the North Pole. They are one of eight species of bears in the world. The only continents with no native bears are Australia, Antarctica, and Africa.

over a hole in the ice. Seals swim under the sea ice, but they must come to the surface to breathe. When a seal pops up for air, the bear grabs it.

After a meal, polar bears wash up. For polar bears, keeping clean is not just about looking good. A clean coat keeps bears warmer than a dirty one. Why? Polar bear hair looks white to us because it adopts the color of the light that hits it. Actually, it is colorless and hollow like a tube. It draws heat from sunlight to the bear's black skin below. This special coat also helps the bears blend into the snowy landscape.

Adult bears have perfected the art of keeping warm. Polar bear cubs need help from their moms to keep from freezing to death.

To prepare for her cubs' birth, a soon-to-be mother bear digs a den. Dens are usually caves dug into earth or snow. They have long, narrow entrance tunnels to keep the mother's warmth from escaping outside. One scientist found a cozy den to be 37°F (20°C) warmer than the outside air.

The mother bear rests in the den for three to four months until cubs are born in the winter. Newborns have thin hair and no teeth. They are the size of a squirrel and depend on their mother for warmth, food, and shelter. They nurse on her fatty milk. The new family stays in the den until early spring, when the cubs are strong enough to journey to the sea ice.

⬆ This polar bear cub rests on top of its mother's head. Mom doesn't seem to mind. Cubs stay with their mothers for up to two and a half years. She teaches them how to survive in their frosty world.

Peek-a-boo! A polar bear peers over the top of an ice floe.

# A POLAR PLACE

Imagine a place where wide stretches of ice go on for as far as the eye can see. In the winter, darkness lasts 24 hours a day. In the summer, the sun never sets at all, giving the place the nickname Land of the Midnight Sun. This is what the polar bears' home—the Arctic—is like.

The Arctic region lies north of the Arctic Circle— a line about three-fourths of the way up the globe from the equator. Inside the circle you'll find the Arctic Ocean, with the North Pole in the center

A polar bear shields his face from a blinding snowstorm.

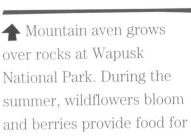

⬆ Mountain aven grows over rocks at Wapusk National Park. During the summer, wildflowers bloom and berries provide food for hungry polar bears.

## HOW TO STAY WARM IN THE ARCTIC

- Three layers of socks
- Waterproof boots
- Three layers of pants
- Two turtlenecks
- Five layers of jackets
- Gloves, face mask, and hood
- Parka

and the northernmost lands of Russia, the United States (Alaska), Canada, Norway, and Denmark (Greenland).

Most of the time, a 6- to 8-foot (1.8–2.4-m)-thick layer of ice covers the Arctic Ocean, which makes it the only ocean people and animals can walk on. Fish, seals, whales, and walruses swim below.

The Arctic isn't where you would want to spend a beach vacation. Below-freezing temperatures and stiff winds are the norm. There are few roads, so when I'm looking for polar bears, I use helicopters, snowmobiles, or dogsleds to get around.

While the land might seem harsh, it is really full of life. In the summer, wildflowers bloom in dazzling colors. You can find beetles, bees, and butterflies fluttering around. Almost 200 different types of birds—from puffins to snow geese—spend the warmer months breeding and nesting here.

What's the secret to surviving the Arctic's cold seasons? Keeping warm. For me, it's not easy. I wear many layers of clothes, a mask, hood, gloves, and waterproof boots. My equipment can also break in the Arctic's freezing temperatures. Sometimes my film gets so cold it shatters like glass in my hands.

A polar bear wanders a rocky coast in Canada while gulls look on. More than 175 types of birds migrate to the Arctic to breed in the summer.

Polar bears are serious swimmers—they can swim distances of more than 100 miles. This mother and cub paddle through the freezing waters of Wager Bay.

A harp seal pup lies on the ice. Polar bears most commonly eat ringed seals, bearded seals, and harp seals. Polar bears can sniff out a seal hiding under three feet (1 m) of ice from a mile (1.5 km) away!

Young male bears play-fight. The bears are practicing for adulthood, when fights over females will be real and the stakes high.

Polar bears do a much better job of staying warm than humans. They have a big advantage: a built-in snowsuit. In addition to their special heat-absorbing coat and skin, bears have a 4-inch (10-cm) layer of fat called blubber. The blubber holds in the bears' body heat and also helps them float in water.

Polar bears have extra-wide paws that work like snowshoes. The paws spread out the bears' weight so they can balance on slippery ice and snow.

Polar bears are designed for Arctic survival. But even so, life in the Arctic isn't easy. These smart bears experiment with different ways to hunt, learn to avoid hunters, and perfect their den-making skills.

When two polar bears meet, anything can happen. I've been entertained for hours by watching young bears play-fight and wrestle. Older bears may fight over food or mates. Their heavily scarred faces are evidence of many battles. Mother bears protect their cubs at all costs from male polar bears and wolves.

Even though their lives in the Arctic are full of challenges, polar bears wouldn't be able to survive anywhere warmer. These bears live up to their nickname—Lords of the Arctic.

A polar bear stares off into the sunset.

# ON THIN ICE

**F**ortunately for polar bears, the Arctic is one area of the world where very few people live. Polar bears have avoided habitat destruction and overhunting, human activities that have landed other bears on the endangered species list.

But polar bears have other problems. Because of a worldwide warm-up, the Arctic ice is melting. In the past 50 years, average Arctic temperatures have increased by more than 5°F (2°C). This may not sound like much, but the heat is enough

A polar bear wanders over a field of ice after sunset in Churchill, Manitoba, Canada. Polar bears are solitary animals, preferring to hunt, sleep, and roam the sea ice by themselves.

77

to melt the sea ice earlier in the summer and cause
it to freeze later in the fall. This shortens the bears'
hunting time on the ice. Without enough time to
hunt, eat, and build up fat, the bears may return to
land weak and thin—and in danger of starving.

⬆ Workers from Manitoba
Conservation—affectionately
known as the polar bear
police—relocate bears who
get too close to people.

78

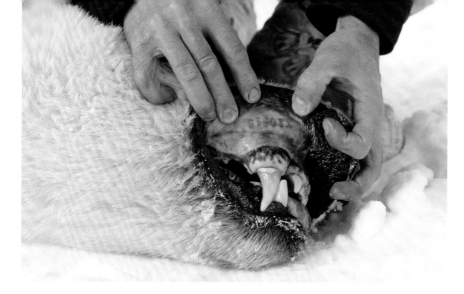

A scientist shows a bear's tattooed upper lip. Scientists tattoo bears, each with its own unique number, so the animals can be identified later.

Scientists hope to learn how polar bears are coping with their changing environment. How do you study a 1,700-pound (770-kg) bear? Very, very carefully. Scientists put the bear to sleep by shooting it with a drug-filled dart. Then they weigh the bear, take blood samples, and give it a checkup. The scientists fix numbered white tags to the bear's ears so it can be tracked and identified later. They also tattoo the bear's number to the inside of its upper lip.

In the past few years, researchers tracking polar bears have found dead bears floating in the water 60 miles (100 km) off the coast of Alaska. The ice melted so quickly that these bears were stranded in the open ocean. They either died from exhaustion or drowned in rough waves and high winds.

Some Inuit hunters have told me that they have noticed changes in weather patterns and currents in

## HOW TO HUNT LIKE A POLAR BEAR

- Hover above seal breathing holes and pounce when a seal appears

- Break the ice to get at young seals below

- Paddle through water toward seals resting on ice, with only your nose and eyes showing

- Follow your nose to find a dead whale, walrus, or caribou

- Watch out for melting sea ice

← In Wapusk National Park,
a mother bear and her cubs
walk across cracked sea ice.
Melting sea ice is a big
problem in the Arctic.

the region. These native Arctic people say that sometimes their feet even sink into melting permafrost (soil that's supposed to remain frozen year-round).

Most scientists believe the recent Arctic meltdown is part of a pattern called global warming. Global warming has been linked to the burning of fossil fuels, which power people's cars, planes, and factories. The burned fuels send gases, including carbon dioxide, into the air. When carbon dioxide builds up in the atmosphere, it can trap heat and warm the planet.

Right now, the world's some 25,000 polar bears are not endangered. But this can change. One study found that in 100 years, the Arctic will likely become 7 to 13°F (4–7°C) warmer. If this happens, the future of the polar bear and its home will be grim. But it's not too late to take action *(find out how on the next page).* It's my deepest hope that polar bears live to capture our imaginations forever. 🐾

# HOW YOU CAN HELP

⬆ Bears can't sign petitions. They need our help to keep their home protected.

Global warming is the biggest threat polar bears face. If too much Arctic ice melts, their habitat will be destroyed. When we burn fuel to make electricity and to heat and cool homes, we add more carbon to the air. Carbon and gases in the air speed up global warming.

■ You can help to slow this process. Try to use less power at home. Turn off the light when you leave a room. Turn off the TV unless you are really watching. If your home does not leak air, you will use less heating and cooling power. Ask your parents to check for tight windows, doors, and good insulation in the walls to prevent air leaks.

■ Some electricity, called "green electricity," comes from wind and solar power. This type of energy does not add to global warming. Your family may be able to buy "green" electricity through your local electric company. Ask your parents to find out about special programs like this.

■ Gas engines in vehicles add carbon, too. Walk or ride a bike to get around, if you can do it safely. Could your family travel on public buses or trains for longer trips, instead of going by car?

■ You can also help to protect polar bears by writing to your senators and representatives in Congress. Tell them you are worried about global warming. Ask them to make strict rules for car manufacturers and to favor cars with better gas mileage, hybrid engines, and all-electric cars. Ask them to support clean-energy development and good bus and train systems.

■ Learn all you can about polar bears and their environment. *(See the list of books and websites in Find Out More on page 115.)* Some animal welfare groups have special programs for young members. Joining a group that studies and works to preserve polar wildlife can be a big help to all the animals.

# IT'S YOUR TURN

Making a snow angel or taking a bath? A polar bear rolls in the snow to clean its fur or maybe just to play.

**Would you like to see and photograph polar bears yourself?** You might find captive bears in a nearby zoo. How will what you know about bears' habits help you get good pictures? Bears do many different things during the day. What would you most like to see them doing? Swimming? Eating? Playing? When do you think is the best time to see each of these activities? How do you think captive bear behavior differs from wild bear behavior? How is a bear's zoo environment different from its natural habitat? You can record your thoughts in a journal and then compare them later against your observations.

**1** Imagine you could study wild polar bears. What behavior interests you the most? What else is there to learn about polar bears?

**2** What would you need to take with you, besides your camera? What else would help you work in comfort in the Arctic? Would you need special clothes? How long would you stay? Would you need shelter? What kind?

**3** You have read that polar bears roam over hundreds of miles during the year. Where would you go to see them hunting seals? What time of year would you see this?

**4** Some wildlife protection groups take kids north to see Arctic animals, including polar bears. Maybe you can go on such a trip—and take your camera along!

## FACTS AT A GLANCE

↑ A cub chews on a twig. Polar bear cubs are playful and curious. They can turn almost any object into a toy.

### ■ Scientific Name
*Ursus maritimus*

### ■ Common Names
Polar bear, ice bear, sea bear

### ■ Population
Between 20,000 and 27,000 worldwide. The International Union for Conservation of Nature and Natural Resources (IUCN) lists the polar bear as a "vulnerable" species. That means that wild polar bears are at risk of dying out.

### ■ Size
Polar bears are the largest species of bear (by record).

### ■ Length
Males up to 8'6" (2.6 m)
Females up to 6'11" (2.1 m)

### ■ Weight
Males up to 1,800 lbs (800 kg)
Females up to 660 lbs (300 kg)

### ■ Life Span
Wild bears live 15 to 18 years. Zoo bears may live longer. The oldest captive polar bear known lived to be more than 40 years old.

### ■ Color
Polar bear skin is black. You can see the skin at the tip of their noses and on the pads of their feet. Polar bear coats look white, cream-colored, or yellowish, depending on the light, but each hair is colorless and hollow.

### ■ Special Features
Polar bear bodies are well built to help them live in the Arctic. Their small ears do not lose much heat. The soles of their feet are mostly covered in fur, to keep them warm walking over ice. They grow a thick layer of fat under their skin that blocks the cold. To help them swim, polar bears have webbed toes on their forepaws. Polar bears don't hibernate like other bears.

### ■ Habitat
Polar bears spend much of the year on sea ice in the Arctic Ocean. A bear may travel across more than a thousand miles (over 1,500 km) on the ice each year. They also roam coastal areas and islands, including parts of the United

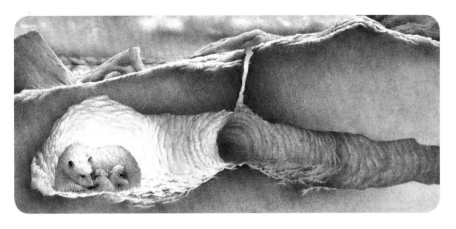

Pregnant females stay in their den from mid-October to as late as mid-April. During that time, mothers give birth to cubs and nurse them until they're big enough to survive the harsh weather outside the den.

States, Canada, Russia, Norway, and Greenland. A bear that lives in one place may roam over 200 square miles (500 sq km) of personal territory.

### Food

Ringed seals are the main food polar bears hunt year-round. They also eat bearded seals, walruses, and beached whales. The blubber (fat layer) is the part of their prey they like best. Near towns and at human campsites, bears look through garbage dumps for food. Like other bear species, hungry polar bears will eat almost anything they can find.

### Reproduction

Bears mate in the spring. Males and females do not stay together. The females find or dig a den in the earth or in deep, hardened ice. From one to three cubs are born there the following winter. Mother bears give birth and raise the cubs alone. Cubs stay with their mother until they are about two and a half years old.

### Social Habits

Adult polar bears usually live alone. At mating time, two or three male bears may follow one female. Mothers travel with cubs until the cubs are almost as big as adults. Cubs from the same litter may live together awhile after they leave their mother. Several bears may share the meat when a whale carcass washes up on shore. Bears living near Hudson Bay in Canada are often seen in groups as they look for food scraps left by humans.

### Biggest Threats

The worst threat to polar bears is loss of habitat through global warming and Arctic development. Bears cannot get enough food when their hunting areas of sea ice grow smaller. Chemical pollution on Arctic lands and in the water poisons bears. Chemicals get into most Arctic animals, including animals that polar bears eat. Polar bears in polluted areas are smaller and weaker. Fewer cubs are born where pollution is high.

# Face to Face | ORANGUTANS

## Tim Laman and Cheryl Knott

NATIONAL GEOGRAPHIC
WASHINGTON, D.C.

This is my wife, Cheryl, following an orangutan through the rain forest in Borneo. It's hard to keep up with them as they move from tree to tree looking for food.

# FACE TO FACE

One day when it started to rain, this big orangutan we call Jari Manis used a leafy branch as an umbrella to keep his head dry. "Jari manis" means "ring finger" in the Indonesian language. We named him this because he is missing part of his finger.

It's not easy to get face to face with a wild orangutan. For one thing, orangutans spend most of their time high in the trees. Also, they are usually afraid of people. But one day in the rain forest of Borneo, I got lucky.

For weeks, I had been following a big male orangutan we call Jari Manis. He had gotten more and more used to me as he saw me following him every day, but he usually stayed up in the trees and kept his distance. Then one day he spotted a treat on the ground that he couldn't resist—a termite nest. Orangutans love to eat termites. He cautiously came down and started feeding, ignoring me. He broke off chunks of nest and sucked out the termites. Yum!

I was there with my camera to record it all. I slowly moved in as close as I dared. I was less than 30 feet (9 m) away from him—the closest I had ever been to a wild orangutan. With my telephoto lens on my camera, I was able to get a close-up of Jari's face.

After Jari finished his termite breakfast, he sat down for a little rest. It started to rain, and then the most amazing thing happened. Do you know what he did? He grabbed some leafy branches from a small tree next to him, and held them over his head to block the rain. He had made an umbrella! That made me realize how smart orangutans are.

Local people realized long ago how similar orangutans were to people. In fact, in the Indonesian language, "orang" means "person," and "Hutan" means "forest." So the word "orangutan" means "person of the forest."

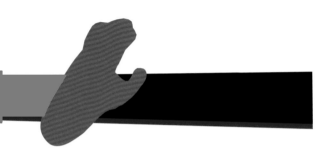

## MONKEY OR APE?

■ Orangutans are great apes, like their close relatives, gorillas and chimpanzees. Monkeys are a different kind of primate.

■ Apes don't have tails, but monkeys do.

■ Apes are bigger than monkeys and have broad chests.

■ Apes have large brains and are very intelligent. They are more similar to humans than they are to monkeys. They are our closest relatives.

As Jari sat there with his leafy umbrella over his head, he looked toward me and our eyes met. It wasn't like looking into the eyes of other animals. It gave me a different feeling, like he was thinking about me. I wondered if Jari knew that his rain forest home was shrinking and that humans were the problem. Maybe not, but I decided right then that I wanted to use my pictures and stories to teach people about orangutans and about saving their rain forest home.

Holding chunks of a termite nest, Jari Manis sucks the termites out of the hollow spaces inside.

This pregnant female orangutan needs to eat a lot of ripe fruits to nourish her growing baby.

# MEET THE ORANGUTANS

Orangutans make a new nest to sleep in almost every night. I climbed about 40 feet (12 m) up a nearby tree to get this shot of a male sitting in his nest before he went to sleep.

**W**hen I was a boy, I loved to climb trees, and I thought I was pretty good at it. But on my first trip to Borneo, I saw a wild orangutan climbing and clambering from one tree to the next, quickly cruising through the canopy. I realized I was a pretty lousy climber compared to him.

Since that first trip more than 20 years ago, I have been to Borneo many times. For several years, I lived in the rain forest doing research and photography. Working closely with my wife, Cheryl,

93

Approximate orangutan range

0      miles     400

0   kilometers   400

SCALE OF ENLARGED ISLANDS BELOW

↑ There are two kinds, or species, of orangutans. One species is found on the island of Borneo. The other species lives on the island of Sumatra. The orangutans shown in this book live in Borneo's Gunung Palung National Park.

who is an orangutan researcher, I have had a chance to learn a lot about orangutans.

The only places in the world that wild orangutans live are the rain forests of two big tropical islands called Borneo and Sumatra, in the countries of Indonesia and Malaysia.

Orangutans spend most of their lives in the trees. They eat in the trees, travel through the trees, and even sleep in the trees. They really

94

In just one day, an orangutan can eat many different kinds of rain forest fruits. These are just some of the fruits they like.

This young male orangutan is eating seeds high up in a giant rain forest tree called a dipterocarp (which means "two-winged fruit" in Latin). You can see the big red wings attached to the seeds—kind of like a maple seed, but much bigger.

depend on trees for their survival.

Orangutans have many special features that make them good climbers. They have long arms that give them extra reach. They have really long fingers to grab on to big branches. Their big toes work like thumbs, so they can also grab branches with their feet. It's like having an extra pair of hands!

The main reason that orangutans need to be such good tree climbers is because that's

**95**

Sometimes Cheryl climbs up to the canopy so she can see the forest from an orangutan's point of view.

# HOW TO SPEAK ORANGUTAN

Orangutans make sounds to communicate. Scientists have funny names for the sounds, like "gorkum," "lork," and "grumph." Here are a few examples:

■ Angry orangutans make a loud "kiss-squeak" sound. You can do this by kissing the back of your hand as loud as you can.

■ Big males make a long call so others know they are near. It starts with a deep burbling sound and then turns into long booming calls.

■ Young orangutans sometimes whimper to call for their moms.

where they find most of their food. Orangutans eat over a hundred different kinds of fruits. They also eat many nuts. But even in the rain forest, they can't always find their favorite foods. Sometimes they can't find any trees with fruit. Then they eat leaves or the inside part of tree bark. Special treats like termite nests are high-protein snacks.

Bananas are one fruit you won't see wild orangutans eating. Bananas don't grow in the rain forest where orangutans live. So if you ever see a picture of an orangutan eating a banana, you know the orangutan is probably in a zoo or was given the banana by a human.

To learn more about orangutans, Cheryl collects some of their urine (better known as pee). This can be a little tricky to do, because they're up in the

Cheryl collects urine from a plastic tarp. She'll take the sample back to her lab to examine it. The urine will tell her a lot about the health of the orangutan.

trees, and you are down below. You don't want to be peed on by an orangutan! Since orangutans sleep in trees, the secret is to put a plastic sheet under their nest early in the morning. Then, when they wake up and pee, you can catch some of it on the plastic. Cheryl later examines the urine to see if the animal is healthy or if a female is pregnant.

This wide-eyed young orangutan is about one year old.

# ORANGUTAN LIFE

O rangutans have pretty big bellies, so it is often hard to tell if a female is pregnant just by looking at her. But one day, Cheryl tested an orangutan's urine and found out she was pregnant.

Having a baby is a rare event in an orangutan's life. A mother orangutan needs to keep nursing her baby for many years and has to carry it all day. So she can't have a second baby until the first one is about eight years old and can travel on its own. No other mammal takes so much time between babies.

This infant orangutan is only a few weeks old. Even newborns are strong enough to hang on to mom with their hands and feet while she moves through the trees.

Baby orangutans cling to mom at first. Then they start moving about on their own. They learn how to use the vines and branches that surround them in the rain forest—their very own jungle gym.

We followed the pregnant female every day so we could see her baby when it was born. It was hard to keep up with her. She traveled farther and farther from our camp, and we had to hike a long way in the dark every morning to get to her nest. One day it rained so much that the streams flooded, and we had to wade through water up to our chests to get back to our camp. Finally, one day she hid so well up in a big tree that we lost track of her. The next time we saw her several days later, she had a brand-new little baby clinging to her.

Females raise their babies all by themselves. The females have to nurse the babies and travel around the forest looking for fruit to eat. Unlike their ape relatives, the chimpanzees and gorillas, orangutans don't live in groups. Except for the moms, who stay with their babies, both females and males are mostly solitary. They live on their own in the forest.

Orangutans do occasionally meet other orangutans, though. Sometimes, if a really big tree has lots of fruit, a bunch of orangutans will gather to eat. Females will sometimes hang out there and even travel together, especially if they are related.

There are two types of adult males, big males

A mother orangutan can have a young baby and also an older brother or sister. They stay with the mother until they are between 8 and 12 years old. For this orangutan family, it's nap time.

## HOW TO STUDY ORANGUTANS

It takes many days of searching the forest to find an orangutan. Here are some of the things you need to do:

- Hike through thick forests, wade through swamps, and climb steep hills. If it starts raining, put on your poncho and keep going.

- Watch orangutans with your binoculars.

- Take lots of notes about everything the orangutans do.

- Get up before it's light so you can get to their nest before they wake up.

(the ones with cheek pads) and small males. All males start out as small males. Some develop cheek pads and become big males right away. Others stay small for many years, and some may never become big males. Scientists are still trying to figure out why this is. It's possible that by staying small, the small males can avoid conflict with other males.

These small males sometimes form little gangs that roam from place to place. The big males don't like each other at all. A big male sometimes gets into a fight with another male to stop him from mating with the females in that area. Males will hit, bite, and wrestle with each other in the trees or on the ground. Sometimes they get injured from these fights, so the life of a big male is a rough one.

Scientists are still learning about orangutans. For instance, we have found that orangutans have different habits, depending on where they live. They may eat the same foods but in different ways. Some use sticks as tools, but others don't. In some places orangutans make pillows and blankets out of leaves. Just as people in different places learn customs from the people around them, orangutans learn things from the other orangutans in their area.

← This man is floating a raft of logs down a river in Borneo. These trees were cut down inside a national park, which is not allowed. Indonesia is trying to stop the illegal logging, but the practice continues.

# THE FUTURE

For many years, we have worked in a national park in Borneo called Gunung Palung. Our research camp is a whole day's journey up a small river, deep in the rain forest. It is usually a peaceful place. But one day, we heard a strange noise in the distance. It was the roar of chain saws echoing through the forest. People were not supposed to be cutting trees inside the park, but they were doing it anyway.

Logging is a huge problem for orangutans in many parts of Borneo and Sumatra because it destroys

← Unfortunately, hunters sometimes shoot a mother orangutan and capture the baby to sell as a pet. Orangutans may be cute pets when they are little, but they make terrible pets when they are strong, fully grown adults. Keeping orangutans as pets must be stopped.

Logging is a huge problem for orangutans because it destroys their forest home. These logs in Borneo have been cut and then pulled out of the forest on wooden tracks.

their forest habitat. Once a rain forest is logged, it is often burned and turned into an oil palm plantation or some other place where orangutans can't live. This is the biggest reason that the number of orangutans has been declining for many years.

Some people kill mother orangutans and take their babies to sell as pets. This is illegal. When local officials find these baby orangutans, they bring them to places called rehabilitation centers.

I visited one of these centers a few years ago. I was shocked at how many young orangutans they had. There were hundreds of them. And the sad thing is that the number of orangutans forced out of their forest homes keeps growing.

At rehabilitation centers, people raise the young orangutans. They try to teach the animals the skills they need to live in the forest. Hopefully, many of these orangutans will be able to live on

↑ Rehabilitation centers like this one in Borneo can get crowded because there are so many orphan orangutans. This is a far cry from life in the wild.

their own one day, but it is hard to find areas of good forest to put them in. Also, it's difficult for people to teach them everything they need to know. Wild orangutans spend about ten years learning from their mothers what to eat and how to survive. A crash course at a rehab center can't fully prepare a young orangutan for life in the wild.

The illegal logging in Gunung Palung seriously damaged parts of the park. But thanks to efforts by the national parks office, the Indonesian government, and conservation groups, the logging has now mostly stopped. The park is much better protected. So there are signs of hope that rain forests can be saved.

To have a safe future, orangutans need large areas of forest where they can live in the wild. That's why we need to protect the rain forests. By doing that, we save not only the orangutans, but all the other plants and animals of the rain forest too. If we work together, we can do it!

# HOW YOU CAN HELP

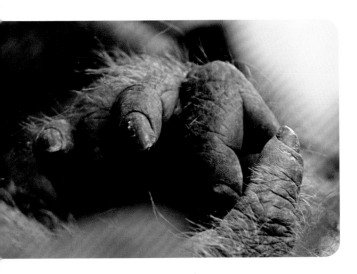

⬇ An orangutan's hand looks a lot like a human hand.

Orangutans live in rain forests that may be very far away from you, but you could be contributing to the destruction of these forests in ways you aren't even aware of.

▬ When your parents buy products made of wood, such as furniture, ask them if the wood is certified as sustainable. This means that rain forests weren't destroyed to get the wood.

▬ Palm oil is used in many of the products we have in our homes. The demand for palm oil encourages loggers to clear the rain forests and plant palm trees instead. Look at your bag of cookies, your ice cream carton, and your shampoo to see if palm oil is used. Ask your parents to try to avoid these products.

▬ You, your friends, and your parents can contribute to one of the organizations working to save orangutans in the wild. National Geographic's Conservation Trust, the Orangutan Conservancy, the Borneo Orangutan Survival Foundation, and the Sumatran Orangutan Conservation Programme are some of the groups helping orangutans. Even if you can only give a little, it will feel good to contribute. Organizations like the Gunung Palung Orangutan Project work with Indonesian children and adults to teach them to protect the rain forests that surround their villages. You can also give to a rehabilitation center that helps the babies who have lost their moms.

▬ Many zoos have important partnerships with orangutan conservation organizations. When you visit these zoos, you help support conservation. Encourage zoos that don't have such programs to contribute to conservation efforts to save orangutans in the wild.

▬ Write to your representatives in Congress and tell them that you support legislation such as "the Great Ape Conservation Act." This act provides funding to organizations helping orangutans and other apes.

## IT'S YOUR TURN

Your best bet to come face to face with an orangutan yourself is to visit one of the many zoos that care for these animals. If you're lucky, you might one day go to Indonesia or Malaysia and see an orangutan in the wild or at a rehabilitation center. Here are some ideas for ways that you can get closer to orangutans:

**1** Visit a zoo with orangutans and plan on spending a good chunk of time at the orangutan exhibit. The longer you are there, the more likely you are to see some interesting behaviors. Have your camera ready!

**2** Think about what is different about the behavior of orangutans you see in the zoo and what you've learned about wild orangutans. Would you see the same kind of social group in the wild? Are they sitting on the ground or up high? What are the orangutans eating? What are they spending most of their time doing?

**3** When you see a movie or commercial that has an orangutan or other ape in it acting like a person, how does it make you feel? Are they showing how the orangutan really lives? Or are they making fun of orangutans by pretending the animals are like people? What do you think they had to do to get the orangutan to act like that?

**4** Learn more about orangutans and the rain forest so you can tell people why it is important to protect them and their habitat. Find out about the different projects that study wild orangutans and about the organizations that are working to protect them.

⬇ It would be fun to be able to climb through the treetops like an orangutan.

# FACTS AT A GLANCE

⬇ Orangutans' feet are different from humans' feet. An orangutan's big toe works like a thumb.

### Species
There are two species of orangutans living on different islands in Southeast Asia. The species living on Borneo is called *Pongo pygmaeus*. The species living on Sumatra is called *Pongo abelii*. They are very similar and were considered the same species until recently. In this book we talk about the Bornean orangutan.

### Population
Today, fewer than 6,600 orangutans live in Sumatra and fewer than 54,000 live in Borneo. Orangutan populations are rapidly declining. Both orangutan species are endangered.

### Types of Males
There are two types of grown-up male orangutans. Big males are much larger, have cheek pads (also called cheek flanges), throat pouches, and make loud "long calls." Small males are smaller and do not have these special features. Small males may develop into big males, but some stay as small males for a long time. Scientists are still trying to learn more about these different types of males.

### Size
Females weigh about 90 pounds (41 kg). Big males can weigh 180 pounds (82 kg) or more. Small males are about the size of females or a bit larger. Orangutans are about 4 to 4.5 feet (1–1.3 m) tall.

### Life Span
Orangutans can live to be over 50 years old. In the wild, it is probably more common to live to be 30 to 40 years old.

### Special Features
Orangutans are the world's largest arboreal (or tree-living) animals. They have hip joints that are like our shoulder joints, so they can move their legs all around, the same way that we can move our arms. This means they can easily stretch between two trees. Orangutans, especially the big males, often travel by swaying a tree from side to side. Then, when they get far enough over, they grab the next tree and spring across. When a young

orangutan comes across a gap in the trees that is too wide for him to cross, orangutan mothers sometimes use their bodies to make a bridge. The youngster then climbs across the mom to get to the next tree.

Sometimes there is a big fruiting season in the forest, called a mast fruiting. When this happens, the orangutans can eat so much fruit that they get fat. When there is not much to eat, they use up this fat for energy.

In some areas, orangutans use tools such as sticks to get seeds out of a certain fruit and to eat insects, but in other places, they don't. They also do other odd things, like making leaf pillows or blankets in their nests.

### Habitat

Orangutans live in tropical rain forests. They prefer to live in peat swamps and lowland forests. Sometimes they go into mountain forests. Orangutans, especially males, have large home ranges.

### Food

Orangutans are known to eat hundreds of kinds of plants. They prefer to eat fruit, including seeds, when they can. They will eat leaves and the inside of tree bark when they can't find fruit. They also eat insects, especially termites, and flowers.

### Reproduction

Orangutans give birth only once every eight years or so. This is the longest birth spacing of any mammal. Pregnancy lasts eight and a half months—almost as long as in humans. Both types of adult males, the big males and the small ones, can mate with females.

### Social Habits

Orangutans are mostly solitary. This means they live alone, except for the mothers and their babies. The big males with cheek pads avoid each other. Sometimes they get into fights. They can even die from the wounds they get in these fights. At times, the small males travel together in groups. Occasionally, a few pairs of mothers and babies will feed together in large fruiting trees. If there is enough fruit to eat, small groups of related females will travel and eat together. In some places, orangutans can be much more social, probably because that place has more for them to eat.

### Biggest Threats

Bornean orangutans are endangered, and Sumatran orangutans are critically endangered. Endangered means an animal faces a very high risk of becoming extinct in the wild. Critically endangered means the animal faces an extremely high risk of becoming extinct in the wild. The biggest threat is rain forest destruction caused by logging (both legal and illegal), conversion to oil palm plantations, fire, and mining. Orangutan mothers are also killed to obtain infants for the illegal pet trade. In some areas orangutans are hunted for food or killed for other purposes. Most orangutans live outside protected national parks, but threats exist even in areas that are protected.

# GLOSSARY

**Adapt:** To become suited to one's surroundings. Animals can adapt to changes in the environment over many generations.

**Alpha:** The highest-ranking wolf in a pack.

**Arboreal:** Living in the trees.

**Canopy:** The top level of the forest.

**Carnivore:** An animal whose diet is based on meat.

**Clambering:** Using both your hands and feet to climb; scrambling.

**Den:** A burrow in the ground or in a cave where wolf mothers give birth and nurse their pups. Adults don't sleep in the den.

**Endangered species:** A species with very few individuals remaining. If the number of individuals rises, the classification may change to "threatened" or "recovered." If the number falls, the species may become "extinct," meaning no individuals are left.

**Environment:** The natural surroundings, including terrain, climate, and other native living things, of a plant or animal.

**Fossil fuel:** Coal, oil, and natural gas. These fuels come from the slow breakdown of ancient plants or animal bodies over millions of years.

**Global warming:** A gradual rise in average temperatures worldwide.

**Habitat:** The local environment in which an animal lives.

**Inuit:** Native peoples in the Arctic areas of Alaska, Siberia, Canada, and Greenland.

**Livestock:** Animals such as cattle, pigs, or sheep that are kept and raised by humans.

**Mammals:** Air-breathing, warm-blooded animals with hair whose offspring nurse on their mother's milk.

**Marine:** Living in or near the sea or ocean, or depending on the ocean's food sources.

**Norm:** A usual state or condition.

**North Pole:** A point at the northern end of the Earth's axis, located in the Arctic Ocean. There, six months of daylight are followed by six months of darkness each year.

**Omega:** The lowest-ranking wolf in a pack.

**Permafrost:** Ground, soil, or rock that stays at a temperature of 32°F (0°C) or below for two years or more.

**Poacher:** A person who takes or kills an animal illegally.

**Predator:** An animal that preys on other animals as food.

**Prey:** Animals that predators eat.

**Rain forest:** A dense forest with over 100 inches of rain per year.

**Range:** The area in which an animal lives.

**Rehabilitation:** Preparing an animal to survive in the wild after it has spent time in captivity.

**Species:** A group of animals or plants that look similar, can breed with one another, and have offspring who can also breed successfully.

**Stalk:** To hunt or track secretly and quietly.

**Subspecies:** The classification just below species. Subspecies live in different geographical areas.

**Telephoto lens:** A camera lens that can act like a telescope, making distant objects appear close.

**Territory:** An area that an animal, or a group of animals, lives in and defends from other animals of the same species.

**Tundra buggy:** A special-purpose vehicle like a bus, used for observing Arctic wildlife safely. Buggies ride high on big tires over ice and snow instead of roads.

# FIND OUT MORE

## Books & Articles

Biel, Tomothy Levi. Zoobooks 2. *Polar Bears.* Poway, CA: Wildlife Education, 1985.

Brandenburg, Jim. *Brother Wolf.* Minnetonka, MN: NorthWord, 1993.

Brandenburg, Jim. *Scruffy: A Wolf Finds His Place in the Pack.* New York, NY: Walker, 1996.

Brandenburg, Jim. *To the Top of the World: Adventures With Arctic Wolves.* New York, NY: Walker, 1993.

Brandenburg, Jim. *White Wolf.* Minnetonka, MN: NorthWord, 1988.

Gamble, Cyndi, and Rodney Griffiths. *Leopards.* Voyageur Press, 2004.

George, Jean Craighead. *Julie of the Wolves.* New York, NY: HarperCollins, 1972.

Hampton, Bruce. *The Great American Wolf.* New York, NY: Owl Books, 1997.

Joubert, Dereck. "Lessons of the Hunt." *National Geographic* magazine, April 2007.

Knott, Cheryl, and Tim Laman. "Orangutans in the Wild," *National Geographic* magazine, August 1998.

Knott, Cheryl, and Tim Laman. "Orangutans Hang Tough," *National Geographic* magazine, October 2003.

Lumry, Amanda, and Laura Hurwitz. *Adventures of Riley: Operation Orangutan.* Bellevue, WA: Eaglemont Press, 2007.

Mangelson, Thomas D., and Fred Bruemmer. *Polar Dance: Born of the North Wind.* Omaha, NE: Images of Nature, 1997.

National Audubon Society. *Guide to Marine Mammals of the World.* New York: Alfred A. Knopf, 2002.

Patent, Dorothy Hinshaw. *Polar Bears.* Minneapolis: Carolrhoda Books, 2000.

Rosing, Norbert. *The World of the Polar Bear.* Richmond Hill, Ontario: Firefly Books, 2006.

Stirling, Ian. *Polar Bears.* Ann Arbor: University of Michigan Press, 1988.

Sunquist, Mel, and Fiona Sunquist. *Wild Cats of the World.* University of Chicago Press, 2002.

## Films

*Be the Creature.* National Geographic Channel, 2004. The Kratt brothers take you to animal habitats around the world. DVD.

*The Disenchanted Forest,* Bullfrog Films, 2002. An award-winning film about returning rehabilitated orangutans to the wild.

*Eye of the Leopard.* National Geographic, 2006. Not rated.

*Life of Mammals.* BBC TV series hosted by David Attenborough. DVD.

## Websites

kids.nationalgeographic.com/animals
*Check out the National Geographic pages on wolves, leopards, polar bears, and orangutans.*

kids.nationalgeographic.com/explore/nature/mission-animal-rescue
*Learn how to help save wolves, polar bears, and other endangered animals.*

animals.nationalgeographic.com/animals/big-cats-initiative
*Get the latest stats on big cats and how you can help protect them.*

animalinfo.org/species/carnivor/ursumari.htm
*Find a polar bear profile and tons of fast facts.*

animals.sandiegozoo.org/animals/leopard
*Learn about leopards at the San Diego Zoo's website.*

awf.org/section/wildlife/gallery
*Meet the leopard and many other animals in the Wildlife Gallery at the African Wildlife Foundation.*

defenders.org
*Find information about wolves' biology and about conservation.*

frontiersnorth.com/the-tundra-buggy-adventure
*View polar bears in the wild and learn about tundra buggies!*

fws.gov/midwest/wolf/aboutwolves/biologue.htm
*The U.S. Fish and Wildlife Service maintains a website on wolves that covers their history, the reintroduction effort, and their recovery.*

greatapetrust.org
*Learn about orangutans and other great apes.*

polarbearsinternational.org
*Learn about polar bear conservation efforts and what you can do to help.*

savegporangutans.org
*Cheryl Knott's Gunung Palung Orangutan Project.*

wwf.org
*The World Wildlife Fund has information on wolves, polar bears, and more!*

## Places to Visit

Polar Bears International has Arctic camps for kids to learn about polar bears and visit their habitats. *For information, see:* polarbearsinternational.org/adventure-learning-program

# RESEARCH AND PHOTOGRAPHY NOTES

## WOLVES

Photographing wolves in the Minnesota woods is a lonely experience. Wolves are most active at dusk, through the night, and in the early morning. This means I have to know where they are, get into position to photograph without them knowing I am around, and then sit patiently, sometimes for many hours without making any noise. Just the process of getting into position is difficult.

Temperatures here range from minus 40°F to 100°F (minus 40°C to 40°C). Because of the cold, my cameras sometimes stop working before I do. Since wolves have such a keen sense of smell, I need to be downwind from them or they will quickly leave. They can even detect the scent of mosquito repellent. Any kind of noise will also frighten them away, even just swatting at a mosquito. Sometimes they hear the clicking of the shutter on my cameras.

People often ask if they can go with me to photograph my wolf neighbors, kindly offering to carry my equipment. But I have found that doubling the scents and sounds usually makes my work unsuccessful, which is why I always work alone. After spending many years gaining the trust of several generations of the resident wolf pack, I am now finding it easier to get closer to them than in the past.

Wolves have been an important part of my life for over 30 years. In the early years of my work, when the wolf population was lower, I was lucky to get one good photograph in a year. Now I see them more often, and they aren't as afraid of people because they haven't been hunted in many generations. If you ever want to see a wolf—get up early, go exploring, and be patient and quiet. —JB

## LEOPARDS

Researching and working in one of the world's most beautiful places is like a dream come true. And for us, a day spent tracking a tiny leopard cub is a perfect day. Each day we find ourselves snapping awake in the dark, usually around 4 o'clock in the morning, eager to get out and find her. We tumble out of bed, pull on clothes already laid out the night before, shake out shoes in case any scorpions have crawled in, and shove all our stuff into steel trunks so the mice don't get in. Then we zip the tent closed behind us, to stop baboons or monkeys from sneaking in and stealing our things. Nowadays, we have to double lock the zippers because they have become so clever!

Then we head out in our jeep. Beverly stands up through a roof hatch, searching, listening to the forest, while I scan the track ahead for the slightest shape of footprints or a movement in the brush.

Legadema has favorite trees to lie in, so we check those. Once we find her, that's it for us for the day. What she does, we do.

Our vehicle is our office, so we keep a lot of cameras spread around, ready for action. We have a section for food, books, journals, hot water for tea, and cold water for the midday heat—which can reach 130 degrees. There is a mosquito net that we couldn't live without. Hats, sunscreen, sunglasses, night glasses for driving when the bugs are out, a sound recorder, and microphones that can pick up a leopard panting at 50 yards. We also have sleeping bags—sometimes in winter it can go below freezing at night.

Our vehicle is our best friend, just as a horse is a cowboy's best friend. Sadly, I don't treat it very well. I drive it in places where no vehicle is meant to go—into valleys of mud that people can't walk through, over rocks to the tops of hills, and across rivers so deep the water comes up over my belt as I sit driving.

This kind of life is not for everyone. But for people who want adventure, it's the best life there is. —DJ & BJ

## POLAR BEARS

What makes a successful wildlife photographer? Some people say the photo equipment. Others say good luck or knowledge of your subject. All are right. But I learned that in the vast Arctic wilderness where the polar bear lives, the key to success is a responsible Inuit guide.

I remember arriving on a remote island in the northern Hudson Bay. My guide, Luke Eetuk, came over and introduced

116

himself. He said: "Don't worry about anything but your photography. I will guide you. I will cook. I will set up the tent. Your job is to create photographs. Your images will tell the people outside the Arctic what our home is all about."

For more than three weeks, Luke kept his word. I never was hungry, cold, or afraid. This is important because a tired body with a hungry stomach doesn't do a good job. Being relaxed, even in difficult situations, is very important for a photographer. Under these ideal circumstances, I feel free to move around, look for different angles, wait for low light, and change lenses as often as I need to.

I photograph with 35mm professional cameras, and I prefer film. My lenses range from 16mm fisheye lenses to 800mm telephoto lenses. To hold the camera steady, I use tripods of varying sizes and, during aerial photography, I use gyrostabilizers.

In the field, there are some challenges that no one can protect you from. In the summer, scores of mosquitoes, black flies, and horse flies, and the inability to take a shower can make life very uncomfortable. In the winter, we grapple with extremely cold temperatures, brisk winds, and 18 hours a day of total darkness.

Why am I doing all this? For the one-of-a-kind experiences! I see animal families acting like us: playing, fighting, having fun, and taking care of each other. I see weather conditions not many people have seen and the aurora borealis lighting up the Arctic during a winter night. Being outdoors is a learning experience. The most important lesson: learning to respect the lives of other creatures. **—NR**

## ORANGUTANS

Photographing and researching wild orangutans in the rain forest is a challenge, but we like it. We get to spend long days outdoors and to see not only orangutans, but also other amazing wildlife. Some things are hard, like waking up before daylight to hike in the dark to where the orangutan is sleeping so you can be there before they get up. Also, working in the rain forest means putting up with leeches, mosquitoes, and a lot of rain and wet boots. But it's worth it.

To get pictures of wild orangutans acting in a natural way, you first have to get them comfortable with you. Even if they are already used to a researcher, a big camera lens might make them nervous. If you take pictures from the ground looking up at orangutans in the trees, the photos often don't turn out well because of the bright sky background. So I tend to follow orangutans when they are in steep, hilly areas. I scramble up hills so that I can look across at their level, carrying a big, bright, 300mm f2.8 lens and my camera. Because there isn't much light in the rain forest, I use a tripod to keep the camera steady.

It's hard to find a gap in the leaves and set up a shot while the orangutan is doing something interesting. Some days I follow one for 12 hours and don't get a single picture. That's frustrating. But other times I am rewarded by a great image of their behavior. I also rig up ropes and climb trees to get to their level. This works best at the big fruit trees where I know they'll visit often.

Cheryl became interested in studying great apes because she was curious about human evolution. Great apes are our closest relatives, so learning more about how the environment shaped their evolution can help us understand our own past as well. But orangutans are hard to find and follow, so Cheryl always works with a big team of Indonesian scientists, students, and field assistants. Her research also inspired her to help protect the orangutan's rain forest home. Her organization, the Gunung Palung Orangutan Project, works with people and institutions in Indonesia to accomplish this. As a professor of anthropology at Boston University she also teaches people about orangutans, apes, and human evolution.

We still have a lot to learn about orangutans and how to protect their remaining habitat. We hope that one day you will join us in the effort! **—TL**

# INDEX

**118**

# CREDITS

## PHOTO CREDITS

**Front cover:** wolf, Jim Brandenburg/Minden Pictures; polar bear, Norbert Rosing; leopard, Beverly Joubert; orangutan, Tim Laman; 1, Mayovskyy Andrew/Shutterstock; **Wolves** (all photos unless otherwise noted): Jim Brandenburg/Minden Pictures; 5 and 22, Joel Sartore/NG Creative; **Leopards:** Beverly Joubert; **Polar Bears** (all photos unless otherwise noted): Norbert Rosing; 85, Robert Hynes; **Orangutans:** Tim Laman

## STAFF FOR THIS BOOK

**Staff for original edition**
Jennifer Emmett, Mary Beth Oelkers-Keegan, *Project Editors*
David M. Seager, *Art Director*
Lori Epstein, *Photo Editor*
Carl Mehler, *Director of Maps*

**Staff for this edition**
Paige Towler, *Project Editor*
Callie Broaddus, *Art Director and Designer*
Lori Epstein, *Senior Photo Editor*
Allie Allen and Sanjida Rashid, *Design Production Assistants*
Michael Cassady, *Photo Assistant*
Grace Hill, *Managing Editor*
Alix Inchausti, *Production Editor*
Lewis R. Bassford, *Production Manager*
Nicole Elliott, *Manager, Production Services*
Susan Borke, *Legal and Business Affairs*

**Senior Management Team, Kids Publishing and Media** Nancy Laties Feresten, *Senior Vice President;* Jennifer Emmett, *Vice President, Editorial Director, Kids Books;* Julie Vosburgh Agnone, *Vice President, Editorial Operations;* Rachel Buchholz, *Editor and Vice President,* NG Kids *magazine;* Michelle Sullivan, *Vice President, Kids Digital;* Eva Absher-Schantz, *Design Director;* Jay Sumner, *Photo Director;* Hannah August, *Marketing Director;* R. Gary Colbert, *Production Director*

**Digital** Anne McCormack, *Director;* Laura Goertzel, Sara Zeglin, *Producers;* Jed Winer, *Special Projects Assistant;* Emma Rigney, *Creative Producer;* Brian Ford, *Video Producer;* Bianca Bowman, *Assistant Producer;* Natalie Jones, *Senior Product Manager*

Since 1888, the National Geographic Society has funded more than 12,000 research, exploration, and preservation projects around the world. The Society receives funds from National Geographic Partners, LLC, funded in part by your purchase. A portion of the proceeds from this book supports this vital work. To learn more, visit natgeo.com/info.

NATIONAL GEOGRAPHIC and Yellow Border Design are trademarks of the National Geographic Society, used under license.

For more information, please visit nationalgeographic.com, call 1-800-647-5463, or write to the following address:
National Geographic Partners
1145 17th Street N.W.
Washington, D.C. 20036-4688 U.S.A.

Visit us online at nationalgeographic.com/books

For librarians and teachers: ngchildrensbooks.org

More for kids from National Geographic: natgeokids.com

For information about special discounts for bulk purchases, please contact National Geographic Books Special Sales: specialsales@natgeo.com

For rights or permissions inquiries, please contact National Geographic Books Subsidiary Rights: bookrights@natgeo.com